This book will break a window if you throw it hard enough.

Markus Almond

Copyright © 2015 by Markus Almond. All Rights Reserved.
Published by Brooklyn To Mars Books

for Susan and Jonas

CONTENTS

Introduction   7

Part One   9

Part Two   55

Part Three   111

Part Four   153

Conclusion   205

INTRODUCTION

Good morning. I got a haircut yesterday from a goddamn lunatic who never learned how to properly use a pair of scissors. I usually cut it myself you know. I play a record, set up my mirror and take my time. But I can never get the back of my head quite right.

Anyway… I hope you enjoy this book. It has many pages. It has a sturdy cover and a good weight to it. Please be careful. The stories here can break your fears and self-limiting beliefs. This book can cause permanent damage. It contains a new collection of stories, quotes and raw confessions. If you don't want to read it, throw it through a fucking window.

-Markus Almond

PART ONE

I want to get a tattoo of you. Maybe I'll trace the birthmark on your leg and get a tattoo of it. But I'll get it on my wrist. I'll do this so when I'm in a meeting or having lunch with some stranger, I can pretend to scratch my arm or look at my watch. And there on my wrist will be the Italy-shaped birthmark that I stole from your inner thigh. And right in the middle of some meaningless conversation, I'll be taken back to those thighs of yours and my tongue dragging across them and wishing I never had to come up for air.

I've been going to this practice space in Greenpoint that rents rooms for $15 an hour. It's in an old run-down building where you have to walk across a fire escape just to get inside. I book an hour or two in studio B and bang away on the drum set. I throw my headphones on and blast through my troubles one rim shot at a time. By the time I leave, I'm dripping with sweat and have the happiest blisters any pair of hands have ever seen.

Did you know that a rainbow is an optical illusion? So if you're looking at a rainbow and I'm looking at a rainbow, neither of us is looking at the same thing. It doesn't exist. It's the light in our eyes. Science is so sad! Fuck science. I say it's a rainbow and we can slide down it if we can catch it!

I want to wake up at noon and make myself a sandwich. I want to eat it in peace next to the East River. I want to go see a matinee and send all calls to voicemail. I want lobster and central air. I want clothes that were tailored just for me. I want to eat and drink whatever I damn well please and sign the bill without looking at the total. I want to live in peace and I want annoying people to leave me alone.

If you can have a fearless attitude toward death, you can do almost anything.

A lot of people have been buying my books lately. I'm not sure if they're actually reading them or if it's more of a "this looks nice on a bookshelf" type of thing. Either is fine by me. If they keep buying 'em, I'll keep writing 'em.

We met in a hotel a few blocks west of Central Park. She brought wine and sex toys and strawberries covered in dark chocolate. We enjoyed a nice dinner at a restaurant across the street from Lincoln Center. She told me about the theatre and we walked on the rooftop made of grass. We sipped the Cabernet Sauvignon from a portable coffee thermos. Then back at the hotel we had drinks on the top floor which looked out over the whole city. I could tell she was tired. But she stayed up with me all night and we fucked like high school kids on prom night.

There are worse things than being scared. There are worse things than nervous breakdowns. There are worse things than getting stabbed in the chest with a prison shank made out of a toothbrush. There are worse things than public speaking. There are worse things than looking like a fool. Living without you is one of those things.

We are just passing through. It has nothing to do with water or carbon or oxygen or the ideal temperature and atmosphere. It could have been totally different and our bodies would have taken a different form. We're just passing through. This world is just dust on our souls. We are not our bodies and we have nothing to worry about.

Your gut knows things. It knows more than the underpaid teachers in the outdated school system. Your gut knows more than your parents who brought you up as best as they could. Your gut knows more than the government or the garbage on YouTube. Your gut knows more than what's written in books or preached in churches. Your gut knows who you love and where you're supposed to be.

I do not want to be the rocky bank that breaks and sends you out into the village. I do not want to be the drought that causes you to dry up and lose your wildlife. I do not want to be a barrel of manmade poison that ruins you from the inside. I want to be oxygen bubbles clinging to your leaves. And I want to be a smooth sandy bottom that gives soft feet a pleasant place to wade. I want to be ripples that ride the smiles and curves of you – the thing that gives you life. I want to be the glacier that paved the way for you in the first place.

I think a good skill is to emit positive energy even when you're surrounded by complete assholes.

You know that scene in every shoot-em-up movie where the hero is shot in the gut and bleeding all over the floors? He makes it through the last 20 minutes of the movie like that – shooting up bad guys with one hand and holding his gut with the other. Life is a lot like that. We've all got our own problems - health problems, money problems, love problems, fears, insecurities, a brutal past that tries to haunt us. But we can't be paralyzed by that stuff. We've got to save the day even if we bleed on the floors.

I've got the Pythagorean theorem tattooed on my forearm. I know secret family recipes for Dutch chocolate. I walk through the back entrances of New York City rock clubs with no questions asked. I have had sex 16 times today. I don't have a cell phone because I prefer not to be reached. The last time I carried less than a thousand dollars was when I was on a motorcycle in Italy and my wallet slipped out of my pocket while doing a wheelie down a back road. I am Markus Almond.

We only get a limited time on this earth. It goes by faster than a punk song in a crowded club on a Saturday night. Stop second-guessing and do things with all of your heart. Trust that intuition of yours and let it fly. You are safe and you will be okay. You will be taken care of by forces that are not understandable by the human mind. There is a safety net under you. Protecting you. Begging you to fly.

The only thing I regret is all the tattoos that I did NOT get.

I am dreaming and you are smiling and running towards my old, beat-up Chevrolet. You don't notice the dents. You never notice the dents. You just jump in the passenger seat and embrace me and forgive me for mentioning that I'd like to see your clothes tossed around in the back seat.

I suppose the wise thing to do at this point is to get ready. Harden up those weaknesses and find a way to overcome those doubts. Start training and get ready for the big fight.

These people want too many things from me. They insist I show up at certain places at predetermined times. And they expect me to return calls and RSVP to things. It's all very annoying and useless. I prefer conversations with strangers or at the very least, some sort of communication where all I need is the smallest excuse and just like that I'm on my way back home and can be with my thoughts again. I like my thoughts. They are good to me.

Some things for artists to remember: Don't use the word "revolution" in a rock song. If you design clothes, make ones that people can wear. If you're just starting out, avoid what's popular (you'll never catch up in time and you'll lose your credibility before you get there). If you're a singer, dress strangely. And if you want to be a writer, seek counseling immediately and consider graduate school in an unrelated field.

They play your song for you in Duane Reade. I have about 7 or 8 songs that are yours. I don't think you know any of them. It's alright. I do a little dance in my Topman shoes and get my box of hair dye. Dark brown. I keep it cool and browse the chocolate bars.

When I was in junior high, some kid brought a gun to school. His name was Kevin. He had giant wire-rimmed glasses. He was laughing and running around and yelled, "It's real! I took it from my Dad's dresser drawer." It looked like some weird collectable antique. The handle had a strange ornate white inlay. It was very small and I would be surprised if the thing would even shoot. But still, there it was - flashed in Kevin's hand at the lunch table and the school assembly – scaring even the bullies and getting all the girls' attention – God how I wanted to make love to those girls – with their black boots and unshaven legs.

I am dreaming in space – floating around up here, looking down, looking out there and trying not to be scared. Oxygen – I brought it with me. Sunshine – 12 hours away. I long for sex and hamburgers. Even a cigarette would be nice right about now. Sometimes I pretend, ya know? Sometimes I pretend I just take a smoke out and light it up right in my bunk or at the console. I hold two fingers up to my lips and take a deep breath. And even now with pure oxygen flowing through my suit, the pretend cigarette seems to calm my breathing and reminds me that everything is okay and I'll soon be home again.

Certain people base their lives around health insurance and vacation days. They marry for practical reasons and talk themselves out of their dreams until nothing is left but a smiling, well-groomed, son-of-a-bitch. They turn into their parents. And I'll be the first to say it – their parents were assholes.

Water needs to move or it will stagnate and this can cause mosquitoes to breed, which may lead to disease. You need to move or you will stagnate. You don't want the blood to stop flowing and you don't want things to become motionless and uninteresting. Poor health and an early death can be avoided by chasing after the thing that brings you excitement.

Doubt is just like a weight on your ankle. There is no use for it. Doubt will only do you harm. Bring with you the things that make you stronger, faster, braver. Adopt beliefs like they are supplies for scaling Mount Everest. Accept ideas that move and bend like a pair of waterproof boots with a firm grip on the bottom. They will get you where you want to go.

We break the rules. We have an escape plan with secret maps to Fiji. We make love in Central Park bathrooms and know how to forage for edible plants just in case we have to spend a couple of months living off the grid.

I don't like these people who call me complaining about things. When presented with a solution it's like they speak a different language. Peace of mind is a concept they've never been able to understand. They bitch about medical conditions and the boss at work and perfect the art of excuses. They viscously defend their right to be miserable.

Self-possession: The state of being calm, confident and in control of one's feelings.

A star just landed on the earth. They're supposed to burn up before they get here. They're supposed to turn into lifeless rocks before they even reach where the radars can detect them. And then they're supposed to burn up in our atmosphere. This one didn't though. It just calmly fell into my back yard – still glowing and melting the grass. I never thought you'd come back. But here you are – beautiful and too bright for direct eye-contact.

Those people you're scared of – they're just as scared of you. That girl that makes you so nervous that you never know what to say – she's just as nervous. The big meeting – everyone else there didn't want to go either. Those times you feel awkward? People love you for trying because it takes the pressure off them.

The important thing is to keep going. We are all going to look stupid from time to time. Don't get wrapped up in it. Focus on mental health and yoga, meditation and large bank accounts. Focus on short work weeks and vacations in Maui.

I don't think it's about working hard. It's about making very calculated decisions. It's about deciding what your time is worth and refusing to accept less than that. You have the right to refuse. And once you learn that, you're on your way.

Some crazy, horrible woman wore your perfume tonight at the bar. I had to get out of there. I just left right in the middle of the band's set. All the guys from the record label were like, "Where the fuck is he going?" But I just walked right out into the street and then down to Union Square and tried to take the 6 uptown. But the 6 wasn't running so I had to come back up and take a cab. I sat in that cab staring out of the window and eventually rolled it down because it was an unusually warm night for March. And I just couldn't get that smell out of my nose. And the way you dressed in school. And that unshaved muff of yours. I didn't know what I was doing but you were my favorite.

The problem with empathy is that you can get sucked into other people's problems. They have a bad day, they get sick, they are upset about something. Humans have this thing in our heads that allow us to feel things that are not actually happening to us. This is why we can enjoy television and books and theatre and sporting events. We can live vicariously. So unfortunately, for the 'victims' in your life, you have to protect yourself. Trust that they will find their own way. Help them as best as you can but do not follow them into the depths of self-pity and inner turmoil.

I respect these people who have dedicated their lives to art. Contrary to popular belief, this path is not easy. It is very difficult. But still they stay the course and become better and better every year.

Sustainability is a profound feat. Anyone can come up with an idea for a business and try it out for a couple of months. Anybody can write a shitty novel. But to survive year after year and keep writing, to keep playing music or tattooing people even when you don't make rent every month, that's how real success is made. That's how shitty writers turn into decent ones.

Time moves much differently in New York than it does in the rest of the Universe. Here, things can happen very quickly. The energy here is much tighter. We are spinning much faster. In a spiritual sense, we live longer lives. We accomplish things that would take five times as long in rural Montana. Careers are launched and destroyed. Fortunes are made and lost all within a two-year lease. We go home for the holidays and relatives look older and fatter and we feel younger. We feel like we just left. And even if we die at age 60, it will be like living to 120 by St. Louis standards. It's true that this place never sleeps. And if we do catch ourselves dozing off too early, we can always run down to the bodega and spend a couple of bucks on whatever it is that keeps our heels in the air.

I'm not sure why I got so scared the other day. I'm sorry I had that panic attack in the woods and swore I was bit by a spider and was about to die right there on the leaves. It must have just been a mosquito. I'm sorry I ran to the car and spun the wheels out – forward and backward and forward and backward again – I thought I was stuck in the dirt or sand until you came running over and yelled for me to turn off my parking break. I don't mean to be so much like a loose cannon lately. I've just never done this before and I feel like I just landed on Mars.

People email me looking for insight. I have no idea. This world moves, you know? What was true yesterday doesn't always make sense today. The people we love sometimes turn out to be assholes. Things change. People grow wings like filthy caterpillars and fly away. Industries collapse. Our children grow old. Some people find a solution in white lies and wine. Others stab themselves with religion. Me? I don't know. I'm just trying to keep it together and not embarrass myself too badly before my funeral.

My friend Sally sings the sweetest songs and plays her guitar - swinging it around and making funny faces. And all the kids sing along and all the critics sing along and even I sing along when no one is looking. We're just friends but I like her a lot as a friend. It's really not the glamour. There's something more to it than that.

I rented a BMW and headed north towards Albany. I didn't request the BMW. It was all they had left. Still it was pretty magical to plug in my phone and listen to satellite radio while letting the power steering do most of the work. It felt pretty nice opening that sunroof and using the Ace of Base TV screen to back out of parking lots. It was such a nice day that I didn't use the seat warmers. Still it felt good to know that they were there.

I am convinced that death is just a little light switch that some stranger flicks by accident. One minute you're in bed, peacefully reading your favorite book. The next minute, flick.

PART TWO

It's a sign that you've lived a full life when people are telling you to cut out all the sex and adventure from your stories because it doesn't seem realistic.

Keep showing up. Even if you're losing or no one else wants you to be there. If the competition is vicious and things are painful or scary, keep showing up. Be a vicious bastard if you need to. You can be controversial and confrontational. Keep showing up until the water starts to part. Keep showing up until the fuckers get out of your way.

I want you to know that I'm taking my heart back. You've had it for too long now and it didn't belong to you in the first place. You didn't take good care of it – just left it in a box with some old letters under your bed. And even when you saw the corner sticking out while you were vacuuming and your hand grazed it when you were looking for wrapping paper - you never even bothered to take another look at the thing. You just pushed it aside and made the bed for someone else.

I make too much money. It just shows up in the mailbox and I have to find new places to put it. Savings accounts. Stocks. All the retirement accounts are full. I give it away. Music in schools? Sure. Transgender support? Sure. Vacations in Spain? No thanks. I'd rather stay in the apartment and write. I don't have a lot of needs in my old age. It's all a goddamn miracle.

The bald man with tattoos at the Buddhist center pretends to know all the answers. Kids pay $10 to sit there in silence for 90 minutes. Afterwards they ask him questions about anger and clinging and sorrow. Their questions are misguided and his answers are irresponsible. Still, at least they sat in silence for 90 minutes and that's a hell of a lot better than Christianity.

I don't know where life came from. The things we see aren't really there. The real stuff is underneath. It's the deep, deep intuition. That's the universe. If you can get in touch with that stuff, you've got nothing to be afraid of. We are all well taken care of.

It's up to you if you want to fall short. No one is going to make you accomplish the things you wish you could. You could lay around all day and never do a damn thing. You could take a nap or watch TV right now. No one is going to force you to do anything. But momentum perpetuates further momentum. Sometimes even falling on your ass is enough to get the blood moving again.

We get hit in the face by life. We smile with bloody gums where our teeth used to be and keep trying. We have plans for our lives and when the world says 'no' we keep showing up until we get our way. If you stop and accept another person's 'no,' you're missing the whole goddamn point. Nothing is easy and growth comes from pushing when things are the hardest.

Love. It comes to us when we don't want it to, expect it to. It tears our chests open and we pretend it doesn't affect us. We say that we can handle it. But it buries itself beneath our skin until we fall helpless. We wake for it. We hover above our blankets and feel weightless for it. And we know it can destroy us like a lobster in a boiling pot. But we prepare the butter and the side dishes and hope this time will be different. And with a little faith and luck, we may be right. We may have suffered through enough shit to learn how to love ourselves. And once you can do that, the rest of the world will follow your lead.

I don't feel sad anymore. My lungs are clean because I haven't had a cigarette in two years. Sometimes I suck on a pen while I write. I get up to use the restroom and on my way past the mirror I notice that I have black ink all over my mouth and my chin and down my neck. And it's not the kind of ink that comes off with soap and water. It's the kind of ink stain that you have to cancel meetings for. It's the kind of ink stain that makes my wife roll her eyes at me.

I like Christmas shopping with you in New York holiday shops and running all over in the cold. The sun goes down early but there are lights everywhere. We fight the crowds but even strangers seem happy. Hot chocolate and apple cider and handmade everything. It's like seeing the city for the first time.

I don't like cool people. I find them exhausting. They have so many "interesting" things to say - some new band or novella you've never heard of. I throw up in my mouth a little. What are they hiding from under those stupid sunglasses?

We were fucked out of our minds – so many drugs I couldn't decide if there was enough oxygen in the apartment to breathe or if we should open all 7 windows in the dead of winter. I got an erection every time I walked in the living room because of the shag carpet. On quiet nights, we cooked meals at 3 o'clock in the morning – leaving the burner on until lunchtime the next day. Things would get so strange some nights. I'd have to turn off all the lights and ask 20 party people to keep their voices down until the police went away.

I want to fish and learn how to clean and cook it. I want to own land and learn how to turn dead trees into a cabin to keep me warm. I want to explore the terrain and not be afraid to swim naked in a lake of mountain run-off.

I do not fit in with these college students. They seem interested in history and are all a little too eager to take the teacher's word for it.

Some people are looking for that one thing that will save them. Love. Money. Coupons. Everybody is looking for something. I don't know much but I know the more things you chase after, the more unhappy you become.

Work will be there tomorrow. And if they let you go, there are a thousand other places to punch a clock. And if the economy collapses and the banks close, we can always write by campfire and survive off of rice, beans, sex and dreams.

I've learned some things. I've come to understand the importance of letting go and moving on. It is what's best for the soul. To hold on to pain is bad for the heart and shortens lifespans. It's always best to roll with the punches and leave the past in the past. But there is an exception to this rule of mine. And there is an exception to every other rule of mine. And that exception is you.

I'd like to wrap you up in fishnets and make you feel like a plate of dessert.

I walk into the bar and they pour me my usual. Some gin type thing. I don't ask anymore. The only bar around here worth going to is this fake speakeasy that no one knows about. And they keep the place so dark. No one bothers me. They hand me my first one and I take a long hard sip. But these days the dick-punchers follow you. Your work emails are in your pocket. Your dysfunctional relationships are in your pocket. Your wife and your criminal cousin. They are all in your pocket. Ex-girlfriends and naked photographs you never asked for. I'd throw the whole fucking thing into the bar sink if it weren't for the simple fact that I need that phone to write down my thoughts and listen to music on the walk home.

The first time you get hit in a fight, it hurts like hell. The second time hurts just as bad but you're a bit more mentally prepared for it. And by the 5th or 6th, you learn to ignore the shit and hit back. And after 20 or 30 fights, your skin and bones have toughened up. Your muscles are like leather and steel and you know you don't want to get hit, but it's less of a pain and more like a fly that just needs a good swat.

I want to smash a couple store windows on Bedford – not too many – just enough to remind everyone that this is still Brooklyn.

Certainty is an island where the tides never turn and no one comes to visit. If you leave, there's a small chance you will drown. But if you stay, there is a 100% chance that you will die on the island. So build a boat and sail the white-crested waves and allow that comfort zone to stretch and expand bigger than the Titanic. Let it grow to be deep in the ocean with the porpoises and wide to every shore you explore and high as the stars in the sky. And let that bubble grow so big that it encompasses the cosmos and arrives in heaven before you do.

You walk with me in Prospect Park. And you wake me up from dreams that you're in. I cannot see an advertisement for the latest women's fashions without picturing you in each dress. I don't even realize I'm doing it. I don't even realize I'm thinking about you. I just wake up at 4 in the morning covered in sweat with a vivid image of you in a Cole Haan dress that I saw on a poster in the subway. I have work at 9am but instead of trying to get back to sleep, I jump out of bed and run to my typewriter to write you down.

I want to dance with you after midnight. I want to take you to a tiny bar in Brooklyn and play Rock 'Em Sock 'Em Robots. I want to close the bedroom door and stay in there with you for hours.

I've been through all this before. The fights, the broken furniture. The drugs. The crying. The filthy excuses and the eviction notice. The mattress set on fire – not in a figurative manner but in the way that ends with a call to the fire department. And in the morning there it is - charred, half-black and impossible to carry now that the water has soaked in.

I have to be an optimistic thinker. Because when I think of the negative, I am drawn to the negative. It's like when you're in a car and you start spinning out of control on black ice after the sun goes down. If you start looking towards the guard rail or the trees you're gonna smash right into the fuckers. Nope, the best thing to do is to ignore all that stuff and concentrate on the white lines pointing home.

I don't like it when I work and work and work and nothing happens. I would prefer it if I had very little effort and got the result that I was after very quickly. I would very much like it if I walked into a bar and the staff politely asked all the annoying people to leave. I would prefer a checking account that was virtually unlimited and a sexual relationship that was always in the mood.

Life is too damn short for television.

I got rid of my used paperbacks last weekend. It was too much to carry around. I took them to Molasses Books and traded them all in for a bunch of wine at the bar. They were first editions but the owner didn't seem to notice. He checked them in and only gave me $3 bucks each. I didn't mind. If he had paid more, I would have been too drunk to walk home.

In this life, we've got to let some things go. As we grow out of our teens and into our 20s we learn how to let go of the shitty things. We quit those part-time jobs. We raise our dating standards. We get away from the people that hurt us. Even that is difficult. Even leaving painful things can be scary. But when we get older, we have to let go of things that aren't so bad. We have to stop doing things we like so that we can give more time to the things we love. We let go of flings so that we can marry soul mates. We part ways with amusements so that we can embrace our obsessions. We toss hobbies aside to live a more refined kind of happiness.

I don't like it when my mind races around so much. But there is no point in trying to fist fight a tornado. I sit calmly and wait for the trouble to pass. I accept the ruthless carnage and inevitable damage. I watch it go by. And when things are calm again, I rise from the stairwell and clean up the mess.

There are some things I'd like to accomplish before I die. But at a certain point, you begin to appreciate the little things. You are healthy and your family is healthy and all of the people important to you seem happy enough – and at a certain age, you know deep in your heart that this is a miracle and you are incredibly lucky to be upright.

We need little successes. We need little stories to recall to help us paint a picture of ourselves that motivate us to keep going. Collect small successes. Get a bunch of them before you take on that master challenge. Make a reputation for yourself before you even show up at the big meeting. It can take years, but the small successes are the only way to get started. They are the snowball before the avalanche.

My wife gives me shit for not reading the news. It's not my problem what these people think is news. Some politician stole money and entire nations are shooting at each other. I trust there are enough college students to protest the nonsense so I focus on what I can control.

I dig up worms for the kids. If they want to learn how to fish, they've got to learn how to bait a worm on a hook. I love them more than anything I've ever encountered before. They don't know about the conveyer belt. They don't know that I am leaving before them. Today they just know that there is a lake and we are under the sky and there are fish and we are going to catch them.

I am passing through this place. Life is just saran wrap that sticks to our invisible soul while we're on our way somewhere else. But it's fun. It's fun to play with. It's fun to pretend that we are the saran wrap. Death is the funniest because when the saran wrap falls off and stops moving, everyone thinks you just vanished. It's a mean joke but they figure it out when their own saran wrap slips away.

I know you bury your emotions 6 feet underground but you're living in a flood zone and those bodies are gonna float into your living room every time it rains.

I got this girl callin' me. I got this guy bothering me. Work stuff. Dumb stuff. I turn off my phone and go read a book by the water. I call in sick to work because I need to focus. I need to find balance in my heart before battle. I need to be strong and streamline my efforts. Everything else is on hold while I sail to the moon.

You wouldn't last a day in my head. You wouldn't know how to breathe in there. You'd get scared every time the sky changed color. And even if you learned how to speak the language you wouldn't know what to say - because the customs are different in my head. In this place love means you stick with someone no matter what. And you fight for what you believe in even if you know it won't end well. And music is more important than money and sex isn't dirty and religion is just as bad as automatic weapons. In my world, children are smarter than adults and love means you stick with someone no matter what.

I think of Kalila in the daylight. That olive ass with tight skin and tiny little hairs that you have to be very close to see. You basically have to have your face pressed up against her to see those tiny little hairs sticking out of goosebumps in the sunlight when a cool breeze comes through the window. What a perfect blend of colors and textures and subtle movement.

I took my work email off my phone. I am an overachiever but not at the wrong things. Sometimes you climb the ladder for years and find out it was leaning up against the wrong thing. When this happens, the best thing you can do is build a hang glider and sail to where things seem more promising.

There are sticky things on this earth. Cigarettes and alcohol. Sex with strangers in the bathroom at Saint Vitus. Anger, sugar and red meat. These things can cling to us and drag us down. It takes some confidence and genetic luck to avoid these terrible tar pits of the soul.

There was a time when I was in jail and drinking too much and the government took my driver's license away. But you brought me home to your parents even though I had tattoos and a piercing in my lip. You helped me wake up for work on time. And when the day came for me to take my driver's test with sober blood, you lent me your car and said, "Don't worry babe. You'll do great."

Has anyone won the free will argument yet? Like if I google, "Free will vs. Fate," will there be some answer like, "Science has determined that human beings indeed control their own destiny"? Or maybe the other side won and Wikipedia declares, "Free will is an illusion and every thought you have, every choice you make, every feeling, urge and sensation were already predetermined and scientifically predictable based on genetics, life experience and the environment around you at this moment." Either way, it would be great if someone posted the answer on a message board or something. Then I could either get to work taking over the world or chill the fuck out and re-watch Breaking Bad on Netflix.

I can never sleep when she's gone. I toss and turn and toss and turn and sometimes I toss and don't even turn. And other times I give up all together and stare at the television. I'm useless in the day time. Woe is me when my wife leaves the city. She comes back and I'm fast asleep before she can even say she missed me.

Money and energy are two different things. I've seen one of the most popular bands of the year fill a club, rock the socks off of everyone, get 5-star reviews and go home and work at a café. I've seen the most boring man alive collect enough private investments and securities to quietly become a millionaire and bore the eyelashes off of every woman within 20 yards. Money and artistic energy are mutually exclusive. I have no advice for this phenomenon. I only wish to point it out so that you are prepared for the poor liquidity of fame and glamour.

Life moves fast. These distractions can really fuck us up. The drinks and the people and the urgent situations. Everyone always seems to have an urgent situation. None of it is urgent. It's all just children pretending to act out their own television dramas and role-playing games.

We're bouncing off of each other. Be careful of who you keep around you. Bounce off the best ones. Bounce off the ones who hold themselves to high standards. Run with the Godsteppers.

I'm always checking my receipts. I went to buy vegetables for juicing. Get a receipt for that! I had to buy a subway ticket to get to the store that sells computer ink. Get a receipt for that! I come home and scan them into a file that says, "tax deductible." But I wonder if I can claim all the time it takes to manage and record these goddamn receipts.

I won't let you go. The floor could drop out on us both and we could be falling to China or the burning pits of hell and I won't let you go. The earth could stop and send us all into space without an ounce of oxygen or gravity and I would hold you tight and won't let you go. Earthquakes and forest fires – won't let you go. World wars and genocide – won't let you go. The worst mistake you could ever make and I still won't let you go.

I get heart palpitations when you call my cell phone. I run to the bathroom and slather my head with hair gel when you say you are coming over. I have never washed my sheets so many times hoping that they are fresh on the nights you end up here. I keep grapefruit in my refrigerator because you mentioned it in passing once. I don't even like grapefruit. I keep waking up earlier and earlier and brushing my teeth more than usual. I am a cool guy and you make me batshit fucking nuts.

I step out of the plane and surrender to the wind. I let the white clouds carry me. There are negative people down there in the mud, whispering that I'm no good. But there are birds up here that sing Chopin and palm trees ready to place cool glasses of coconut juice in my hand. I succumb to the idea that I am tiny and the universe is infinite.

PART THREE

I like that you're a fan of willow trees. I like that you enjoy picnics in Prospect Park. I like that you buy dandelion wine from the farmers market - not because of the taste but because you like the bottle. It looks nice in the kitchen and is the perfect shape for holding olive oil.

All you need in life to be happy is your values. If you can hold on to those, you'll land on your feet like a fucking cat in Doc Martins.

Sometimes I wonder what it would take to get you back in my mornings.

There was this feeling of discomfort and uncertainty after I met you. I was very uneasy thinking about you out in the world - riding the subways without me. I lost sleep thinking you were out there somewhere – dozing off without my hand on your ass.

I will take you as my midnight laugh partner, morning couch hugger and all around closest friend. From bottle service to ziplock bags of dimes, from body builder to Stephen Hawking. I promise to catch you when you slip on icy sidewalks and cook your dinner when you forget how. I promise to always have trouble sleeping when you are out of town. If you should pass away before me, I promise to start a charity organization in your name and smoke several packs of cigarettes a day so that we may meet again sooner.

People run around and God bless them, they think the details are important. People attach themselves to temporary outcomes like it's a matter of death. If everyone stopped what they were doing for a second, took a deep breath and looked at each other, I mean really looked at each other, we'd understand that love and community are far more important than arguments or staff meetings.

I sleep on Hawaiian beaches and smoke cigars made in Europe. I eat deli meat that was prepared a mile from here and tell stories to a native girl who believes that I am high on drugs. We have a mutual goal of avoiding work and getting sun. We enjoy snorkeling with turtles and making love in sheets that were changed this morning. You will not catch me in a stressful mood anytime soon.

If you have a muse, protect her. If you have a fear that drives you, let it. If you have a drug problem, find a balance. And if you're so out of control that you don't know up from down, build a space station in your mind where you are safe and the earth below looks beautiful and warm.

The things we believe about life after death deeply affect how we act on a daily basis. And how we act on a daily basis directly affects what kind of life we have. So don't choose the beliefs that are the most realistic. Choose the beliefs that enrich your life.

I write in the daylight. And the world is spinning out there. Families are walking in the park and bros are having bar-b-cues. Beautiful women are sunning themselves on the greenest lawns and I am typing away, unshowered and unshaven, with tiny rays of sun sneaking through the shades.

I guess I'm supposed to be thankful when people buy my books. I guess I'm supposed to be happy that people are interested. I guess there's something wrong with me because I don't give one goddamn about any of it.

Life is complicated, man. People are moving, living things. Souls can bend and dance in the wind. What we wanted yesterday doesn't always hold true. But one thing's for sure, everything has a shelf-life, from the people we love to our favorite song. Our perception of such things change every time the sun goes down.

I am a spinning planet. I get hit with asteroids in the form of business calls and emails. These things can knock me off course if I am not careful. But I know my density is vast and my trajectory is my choice. I will orbit whatever sun I damn well please.

We laugh in bed because we are happy in love. We put our struggles aside after a long workday because we know it's better if we're happy. We take care of each other and laugh whenever possible, not because everything we do is funny but because these giggles make things feel light and exquisite.

There comes a strange slow flood in the veins when you stick to something - whether it's writing or performing or building a cabin and living in the woods. When you do something year after year and don't let the dumb fucks dissuade you, there comes this invisible confidence that begins to seep in. It starts in your toes. And then it moves up into the ankles and knees. And eventually you're walking down the street and you are well-protected by the stuff. Nobody can see that ocean of strength in your bones. But they can sense just by looking at you that they better get the fuck out of your way.

You talk about heaven with certainty that I'll be there. But I don't know, I think maybe your upbringing got the best of you. People focused on death tend to miss what is happening in their lives.

A young girl wrote me an email tonight about a spelling error in one of my books. My mom emailed about some family things. And work. The work emails pile in like garbage trucks full of shit after all the sewers have overflowed. They sift the shit, put it in giant strainers. The water seeps out and they take what's left and put it in my inbox. I turn the computer off. I disconnect the accounts from my phone. I dream of Fiji and your naked ass in the sand. I'd taste the salt water on you.

Lately, I've been thinking about starting a Brooklyn To Mars group. We will meet at strange times in strange places and we will be like a secret society that always looks out for each other. Maybe we'll call it the Mars Initiative. And we will meet in Prospect Park and go on bike rides. And we will spend Saturday nights drinking in the back room of some Brooklyn bar that is not open to the public. And we will be pivotal members of society. We will go on to be lawyers and politicians and hedge fund managers. And when one of us becomes President, online chat rooms will be abuzz with rumors that the President of the United States is part of the Mars Initiative. It will be like a real life fight club except no one will fight and there will be a lot more sex going on.

Geez, the checks keep coming. I have to sort them into piles and spend 20 minutes a day endorsing them before I go to the bank. Sometimes I have to go twice there are so many.

I dream of seeing you in an airport one day. I have a layover and you've snuck away from your life for a couple of hours. And I know for sure that you still love me because you bought a ticket to Cleveland just to get through security. And you tear up the boarding pass when you get to my gate because nobody actually wants to go to Cleveland when they don't have to. I walk off the plane half-drunk and still not completely convinced that you'll be there waiting for me. But at the sight of you, I sober up with adrenaline and my suitcase falls to the ground or maybe just feels that way. We make eye contact instantly. We could recognize each other's body language in a fog from across state lines. A friendly hug turns into a previous life flashing before our eyes. Your hair smells the way my dreams used to smell. It takes longer for cheese to melt than it does my soul in that moment. We wander off together to a nearby airport bar. I order two drinks but both of them are for me. And you can't stop smiling. I think maybe you still have it for me because you are smiling so big. I don't think you realize how big you are smiling. And I wish I didn't care so much about appearances because if I had my way, we'd both sit in the same booth and instead of gazing across this table, I would put my hand on your knee and kiss you on the lips. In a perfect world, flights are cancelled and airport bars never close.

I just want to stumble to bed and rest my head on your chest because sometimes touch means more than words and tonight is one of those nights.

Let the critics write about how they thought the world should have been. Let them plead and beg uninterested 'readers' to buy into their version of art - the one they studied in classrooms. Let them feel tall and mighty - attempting to throw tomatoes at bleeding dogs. At least the dogs had the guts to fight.

Maybe I was a little crazy when I was young. But you were running all over the place and I had things to do. I had countries to see and music to make. And not you or your good intentions or atomic smile was going to stop me. You melted me across seas and I always wandered back just in time to watch you leave again.

Sometimes the love of your life shows up at all the wrong moments. Maybe you're in the middle of a fender bender and she strolls by on the sidewalk and gives you a wink. You want to go and talk to her but the guy standing in front of you says, "I'm gonna need your insurance information." Or maybe she shows up when you're just a kid floundering around - a teenage mess not even sure who you are yet. Nevermind trying take care of anything other than pimples and gym shoes.

People think art belongs in a museum. They get very upset by anything offensive or morally challenging in the real world. They want a frame around it and a little white sign explaining why it's there. So when you order three tall boys of sticky malt liquor and spin them around on the dance floor like a human carbonated sprinkler and get all the girl's dresses and the DJ booth full of carbonated puddles, they don't call it art. They call the police.

I don't work out to look good. I work out so I can pick fights with douche bags who order bottle service and hail cabs by stepping out into the street. They wear very baggy jeans and always seem surprised when the weird, pale writer punches them in the face.

I miss manual faders and analog mixers. I miss little mistakes and quirks on albums recorded to tape. I miss those strange moments that make a man wonder, "Was that on purpose?" Because for all those imperfections and for all those small awkward nuances, the sweet spots sound heavenly because you know that they're real.

Sometimes I feel like I can't keep it together. But Conrad said to, "Never show urgency, irritation, or uncertainty." And this has been a mantra of mine in the past few weeks. To keep it together. To pretend everything is fine. Because if I scream in a panic now, we'll all be broke before sunrise.

I don't like the springtime. My most productive season is winter because it gets dark so early. And I get manic at night. I write entire novels while everyone else is asleep. So when spring comes and we gain an hour, I get a little disappointed. The sun stays in my kitchen long after dinner and there are more people on the street on my way to the liquor store. I like it when it's cold, when the sidewalks are covered with ice and no one stops to chit chat or sit on my front stoop. "Out the way, son. I got work to do."

Love can throw you upside down. One minute it's here, the next your calls go straight to voicemail. It only takes a couple of days and gravity seizes to exist and you are floating again. You knew it was coming. You even thought about ending it yourself. And you forgot this feeling, this "No one lookin' out for me but me" feeling. And it could take awhile, maybe even 3 or 4 more of these catastrophes before you realize that there is something out there. Call it whatever you want but there is a momentum that carries us through catastrophe and sets us down on a warm beach once in a while. It's there looking out for us.

Yes, you are gorgeous and know how to wear make-up. And yes, any one of us here would be more than willing to take you to bed. But I know that you are a vulnerable girl who used to run around her parent's house in pajamas with footsies connected at the bottom. You would lie on the carpet and laugh so sincerely that even the neighbors would smile at the sight of you. And you are taller and you have molded yourself into a sexy young woman. But you are like the rest of us, still scared and wanting nothing more than to be seen for the true you and being loved for it anyway. You might intimidate the others but not me. I had those footsies too.

Love is a real thing. Sometimes you love somebody for so long you stop seeing the love – like a fish in water. But don't leave – don't ditch the fish with the lake water. Shake things up so you can see the love again. Buy some sex toys and do something weird like take a flying leap towards the sun. Try to breathe up there and your gills won't work. You'll know for sure when you come crashing back, you are a fish and this is love.

I am supposed to take things from the atmosphere and put them on a page like one of those dead moths pinned in a frame for decoration. But those moths had good lives and they were busy doing God's work before some bastard squeezed the life out of their wings just because the colors went nicely in his study. Maybe if we shut the fuck up for a second and listened to the rhythms of the world, we would realize that there are things more important than what goes with our wallpaper. Maybe if we pay attention for a change we'd see that the world would be a better place if we left the moths alone.

The devil lives in a Brooklyn bar and she doesn't like small talk. She just sits there and drinks and drinks and gives people the stink eye. She has an alcohol tolerance higher than a tequila worm. The devil bitches about how the neighborhood has changed and gives everybody a hard time. Every hour, the devil goes into the bathroom to piss and to reapply the make-up she sweated off. We've got her all hot and bothered. Our optimistic eyes make her self-conscious and nervous. We offer to buy her shots and she tells us to fuck off. I ask her to dance and she tells me she'd rather die of malaria.

The world will wash over you like an ocean after you've slipped off your board. And life will keep moving without you. And yes, people love you and they will love you no matter what. But they don't always understand your desires or dreams or hopes of greatness. They love you but they cannot bring you to the surface again. It is up to you. It is up to you to stay focused on the sun and swim towards it while you have a chance. It is up to you to fight through yards of terror and salt water. It is up to you to swim towards the sun until you can get your breath back.

You can't change the people you love. Your best bet is just to stay strong for them. If they ask you for help with their car or want to meet for some coffee, just put your bullshit aside and take care of the bill.

Swimming on the beach is free. Walking and camping in our National Parks is free. Falling in love is free. Meditation and meeting a kind stranger – all free. Working a job you hate for money costs more than your time. It can wear on everything about you: your time, your health, your spirit, your outlook on life and your ability to love. Working for wages will steal your soul. Do not let this happen to you.

Set fire to a Ferrari today.

I want more than strong drink tonight. I want hand guns and targets filled with gasoline. I want explosions on contact – clouds of fire shooting into the night sky. Throw nails on the roads to slow down the cops. The dance clubs and the boat tours and the sparkling lights of New York are no match for you tonight. The bottles don't have enough in them.

PART FOUR

I am chugging whiskey and setting off fireworks in Central Park. I light the wick and move to a different part of the park. The rangers don't know what's going on. They can't find me. It's pitch black in here. I can see their little carts from 100 yards away. They've even got the police involved now – blue and red lights flashing. I light four more and head towards the reservoir.

I wish I could summon you to just appear in this room with me some nights. I just want to hear about your job and your new jeans and what you had for lunch. I just want to make you laugh and hold you in my arms while we're both still alive.

Moon, oh beautiful Moon, how did you get to be up there so big and so blank all of the time. I'm not buying it Moon. I don't think something can orbit that long without getting closer. Surely one day, our rotation will smash so we are spinning in unison. The length of a day will equal a month and the two of us will dance as one.

Fear is a black smoke that can get in your lungs. You can't hold your breath. Just breathe it in and move on. It looks bad but it won't kill you.

These small town memories hit me from all directions and I do everything not to flinch. I had my heart broken on this road. I fell in love with the neighbor girl who used to dance between that sidewalk and the willow tree. Over there is where we had my grandma's funeral. That's the school yard where I got ridiculed for not hitting puberty soon enough. And that dry cleaners is where I worked my first summer job. I fantasized about buying a car and leaving this black hole town.

I sneak into the practice space at 3am. Banging away on the drums the lights flick on. "What the fuck are you doing in here? You can't be in here at this hour." I say, "Ah shit, man. I didn't think anyone would stop me. I just wanted to bang the drums for a bit, you understand." The guy exhales and says, "You gotta come back when we're open. You can't just break in here. That's fucked up, man." I put the drum sticks down and he lights a cigarette. I collapse on the couch and he starts a conversation about music. Some band from Europe left a handle of Jack Daniels and after a couple of hours we finish it - both feeling a lot better than we did earlier in the evening.

There's always going to be resistance in the world. There's always going to be people around telling you to stop – stop being so optimistic or dreamy or ambitious or aggressive. Ignore them.

I had to let my dreams go in order to make them a reality. Most people never give up their dreams. They hold on forever because they know that when dreams turn into reality the magic is gone. I gave up my dreams in order to make them real and see them in the daylight. They are walking, breathing things now. They need to be tended to and they need attention like anything else in reality. They are less glamorous than they used to be. But the thing about giving up your dreams and allowing them to become real is that you get the chance to fill your head with brand new dreams again - bigger and more hopeful scenarios than you ever imagined possible.

It's very lucky that I have kept breathing for this long. I used to leap out of moving cars and run home before they crashed into something. I used to have unprotected sex with entire college campuses. I used to inject drugs right into my neck and do Irish jigs on the edges of government building rooftops. I used to skateboard across highways and sleep in retention ponds and on benches outside of police stations. I used to provoke bartenders and doormen and frat boys and gym teachers and security guards and anyone else who had it coming. I used to smile real big for the camera and ask everybody to dance with me.

Nothing is ever going to be perfect. There are always going to be little annoyances, little worries. But regardless of what happens tomorrow or next week or next year – I love you. And that doesn't come along very often and it's even more seldom for a guy like me. And as I get older, I realize that this shit doesn't last forever. Eventually, our best days will be in our past. Our happiest years, our first choice loves and even the best versions of ourselves will all end up in the past – memories. So I wanted to tell you this. I am in love with you now. And now is all there is.

I'm going to miss Ray Charles and Radiohead. And I'll miss the storage shed. And I'll miss your smile and the way you looked at me back when no one else would. I'll miss the early version of you, the one I met before things went sour. I'll miss that innocent edition of your soul before we got too experienced for our own good. And I'll miss your legs and the way you smelled after a good run.

I write. I'm not saying I have talent. I'm just saying that I write. I'm like a bastard painter frantically spewing oils onto canvas in the basement of the titanic. I am a tourist on Earth - just passing through - taking manic notes and leaving them behind so that maybe one day somebody who thinks like me can read them and slap me a spiritual high five.

When the wife goes to sleep and the friends have already called it a night - when the bars are closed and even the corner bodega is out of cold beer, I am just getting started – my ears plugged into my playlist and my fingertips breakdancing on the keys. When the rest of the world is drunk or asleep or fucking or crying or staring blankly at a television, I am sailing through black ocean waves. And I have one secret that most people will never know about – my boat doesn't sink.

The sun has nothing on me. Hey sun, did you ever think that you need us as much as we need you? Stop being so cocky. Who do you think is keeping you so stable anyway? Sure you're bright and proud and we bask in the glory of your accidental rays. But without us you'd be bouncing around out there without anyone watching. If it wasn't for our living blue circle, you'd be just a useless smudge of gas.

I'll be vulnerable and I will not bring a back-up plan. I will show up with stage fright and do it anyway. I will not cover up or attempt to save face. I will be raw and honest and let them hang me if they should choose to do so.

We were supposed to be invincible. Now we have to worry about cancer scares and sore muscles, strange lumps and high cholesterol. Fuck you, man. We didn't ask for this. Buffalo have shorter lifespans but they don't have to spend the second half of their existence considering sugar intake and exposure to UV rays.

As a writer, the world will pass you by. The musicians will pull better looking women. The actors be more popular. Even the film editors will have higher salaries than the screenwriter. We are a slow whale – sucking plankton and only coming up to breathe every once in a while. The rest of the world will forget about us. They'll plagiarize or rephrase us and claim our wisdom as their own. But we will get by and if we're good enough, we'll be able to afford a bottle of wine every now and again and not have to worry too much about working a real job.

When you're not sure how much longer you can do it, when all you want to do is give up and go back to bed, just shut the fuck up, make some coffee and get back to work.

The other side of fear is where all the successful people live.

If I could tell you one thing, I'd tell you that we are a group of mammals making up stories and rationalizing to each other what life is about and how it should be lived. But you don't have to listen to any of it. You can break the rules – even your own. You can stop doing things you don't like. You can go on vacation and never come back. You can walk out on people that don't make you happy. You can leave situations that drain you. If I could give you one piece of advice, it would be to stop working 40 hours a week, spend more time with the people you love and never use the word "can't."

I woke up today and had these six-pack abs and focus sharper than a Japanese fillet knife. And I had razor-like eyes that could see the world for what it was and who I was and where I was living and where I needed to go. And I didn't even bother saying goodbye. I just bought my ticket and got the hell out of there.

Always be willing to walk away. If you can do that, you will have the upper hand. There will always be other jobs and other relationships and other colleges and other clubs or whatever the fuck nonsense you've gotten yourself into. Don't put so much pressure on yourself. Be willing to walk out of there. Master that and you will find yourself in happy places.

I want to contribute to society. I want to have a positive influence and be well-liked. I want to make love. I want to dump all my alcohol into the ocean and wake up before the roosters start hollering. I want to fall deeply in love with an optimist. I want to stop checking email and feel close to God. I want to write non-fiction books in a hammock for hours and exercise my body without using a machine.

The dame will leave. The dog will die. We will force a goddamned smile. We will dance in bars even if our knees start to hurt. If the rabbits eat our food, we'll eat the rabbits. And if we ever feel down, we'll stand on our heads and say, "Things are looking up."

Stop asking your loved ones to change. You should kiss them on the face while you still can.

Sometimes I smell cigarettes while I am writing in my office. Obviously, this can only mean one thing – there is a ghost standing next to me and he is a smoker.

There is no money in writing. People email me asking me to speak at colleges, asking me to do book signings. There is no money in this. I don't even like the recognition. I never should have used a name. I should have just posted anonymously. I should have taken my face off the back of every book cover and used a woman's name.

Be careful about what direction you're walking. Wander around aimlessly if you want but don't go bitching about how you haven't gotten anywhere after years of walking. Don't walk someplace you don't know about and cry that it's not as good as you thought when you got there. Know what you want, be sure, and go in that direction.

I miss Amy Winehouse, Kurt Cobain and Lou Reed. I wish I could get them all in one room and juice some vegetables together. "Hey Kurt, can you skin this cucumber? Amy and Lou will wash the kale." With any luck, the juice would make them feel so good that Amy and Kurt would quit drugs and Lou's liver disease would disappear.

I think we should own land. As I get older, I've become very uncomfortable with the idea of living in somebody else's building on somebody else's land. Seems like too many things could go wrong and you could be left trying to spend the night on the 7 train with all of your stuff in a bag. Seems like it's a tough world out there and I don't know if my landlord is really paying her taxes or if my neighbors fell asleep with the burner on.

I march out onto the icy sidewalks. I had been in my apartment too long. The walls started to disintegrate in there. Everything turned invisible and I forgot how to sleep. So I venture outside into the cold and walk to the grocery store that is further away – the one with the better produce. And I keep my hands in my pocket and my eyes to myself. I've got all the emotions a human can experience under that jacket of mine - reliving old loves and discovering new spiritual corners of the cosmos. Strangers wouldn't know that. To the average pair of eyes, I'm just a skinny man buying blueberries.

The last time I saw you there were two of you and I was throwing up in the women's bathroom and you were arguing with the DJ and the security team about a missing coat. But I was able to get 3 girls' phone numbers that night and I gave 2 of them to you. I guess it never mattered if we were in the DJ booth or in the back of a police car, things always seemed pretty cool when you were around even in the face of death or municipal court.

These strangers - they don't know anything about us. And for a long time, years even, we tortured ourselves over what they might think of us. But one day we figured it out - there isn't anything real behind those skeptical eyebrows and critical comments. They don't see the fire in our blood when we talk about what we love. They are the poorest people on earth.

Beware of those who seem perfectly happy to do nothing with their lives.

I miss my Uncle Cliff and the smell of lake water. I miss Alhena and the way the corners of her mouth would move when she smiled. But I am a fucking warrior and warriors don't look back too often. Melancholy is nothing but a luxury between battles and I don't like to stay still for very long.

Don't worry about me. I lived a great life and I knew I'd have to leave eventually. You can miss me a little but don't be sad for me – because you've got your own life to live and it's gonna go by very quickly. So get out there and grab on to some things that make you smile. And remember, one day your body is gonna be a thing, not a person. So use that body and have fun while you get to play here.

Remember to emote in moderation and never feel too sorry for yourself. You'll see things through just like you always do and nothing can ever bring you down without your consent.

This moment is peaceful. There is nothing actually wrong right now. There is nothing to be afraid of. Maybe you have the big presentation next week or don't have enough money for rent or have to fly to Texas for that event that you don't want to go to and you need to go to the store for contact solution but you don't have time between your lunch meeting and your big sales call. Just stop. Nothing is wrong in this moment. This moment is peaceful and those other things are just projections. Don't be fooled. Let that stuff go. It will all take care of itself. Those things do not need your attention right now. You are projecting fear onto things that are not happening. Just breathe and enjoy the peace of right now. The stress and the nervousness are just projections from your mind. They aren't real. Let them go.

Abandon secondary missions.

I believe there is more behind our eyes than intelligence and vicious survival. There is something inside us that never dies and that's the part we should dance with more often.

I have been in a constant state of ease lately. I let work go. Now there is nothing making me nervous, nothing keeping me on edge. I gave up shortsighted endeavors. Now there is nothing keeping me up at night. There is no obsession or worry about making some project come together. I clearly define what is important to me and these things are here and now and this is life and I have it.

I hope you will fall in love all over again. And I hope you smile and laugh and feel safe and loved every morning when you wake up. I hope he takes you on camping trips and rubs your shoulders when you ask him to. I hope your children make you feel beautiful and adored. I hope the sun shines on you while you lounge in your backyard and the stars watch over you while you sleep. I hope you think of me fondly but not frequently. I hope you know I love you, but have no sorrow for the way things came to be.

Although I have been drinking, I am not drunk. And although I am not drunk, I did spill red wine all over the bed - and the nightstand - and the table lamp sitting on the nightstand - and the white wall behind the nightstand - and the power box adapter behind the nightstand, with four open outlets - now purple, and hissing, and making the table lamp flicker - like lightning - ready to go off as I wet a towel in the kitchen and wonder whether I should sleep without an alarm clock or next to a purple, wet, bolt of lightning.

I tried real hard to get my shit together. I said, "I'm gonna take a break from drinking and writing and I'm just going to invest in real estate and really focus on my future." Next thing I know, I'm in Puerto Rico throwing up on a piano and getting kicked out of a karaoke bar.

It is a goddamn miracle I have survived for as long as I have.

I woke up. Some bastard broke the curtains at the party last night. Now it's just sun. Sun in here for days. In my eyes and on my clothes. It follows me into the bathroom. It's going to take days to wash all the sun out of here. I'll need several dark nights of seclusion before I feel safe again. Who are these people? Where do they come from - knocking down curtains and eating all the chips?

We must recover quickly and gracefully. We're all going to look like a bunch of dumb dicks from time to time. There's nothing we can do about that. The important thing is get our mental space to a place where we can save face and get back to the chase. Because when we beat ourselves up too badly and start to believe that we're no good, it can be harder to remember just how brilliant we are when we allow ourselves to be.

I would prefer not to do book readings. I type because the midnight earth demands that I record what is on my mind. But it's so embarrassing the next morning. It's like being asked to re-hash the conversation you had while you were stoned out of your mind in the middle of the night. It doesn't make what you said less truthful, but asking some lunatic to recreate his passions and discoveries on command just seems cruel. I write when I feel like it and I am quite boring in the daytime.

I don't like getting my haircut. Where have those hands been? Is she hitting on me? Oh my god, I can't breathe in this apron. It's really tight. My eyes look swollen. Are we supposed to be making small talk? Oh, my god, I'm terrible at small talk. Can she sense my fear? "Okay, so what do we want done today?" Jesus Christ, here we go. No turning back now…

CONCLUSION

Thank you for reading my book. By now you know that I am not a violent man. I was only kidding when I came up with the title for this book. But I don't believe that we should run from confrontation. I don't know if breaking windows is a good idea. But there's nothing wrong with getting worked up once in a while – especially when the only consequence is a little fresh air.

Thank you for everything,
-Markus

P.S. Sign up for my mailing list and get cool stuff at www.brooklyntomars.com

OTHER BOOKS BY MARKUS ALMOND:

Things To Shout Out Loud At Parties
Brooklyn To Mars: Volume One
Marching Band and the Expanding Universe

Made in the USA
San Bernardino, CA
27 June 2017